AF344940
Thank You
for the
purchase.

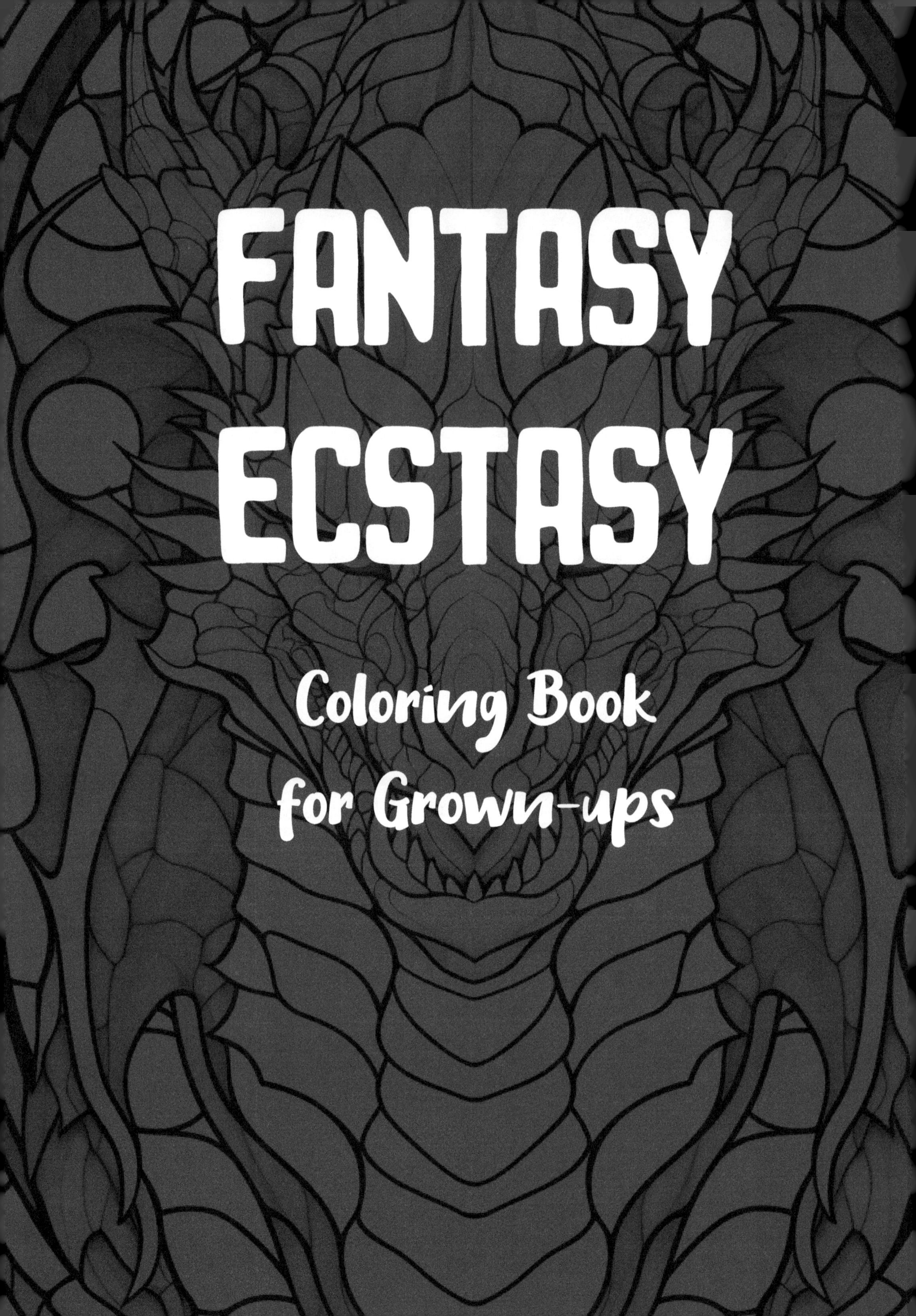

FANTASY ECSTASY
Coloring Book
for Grown-ups

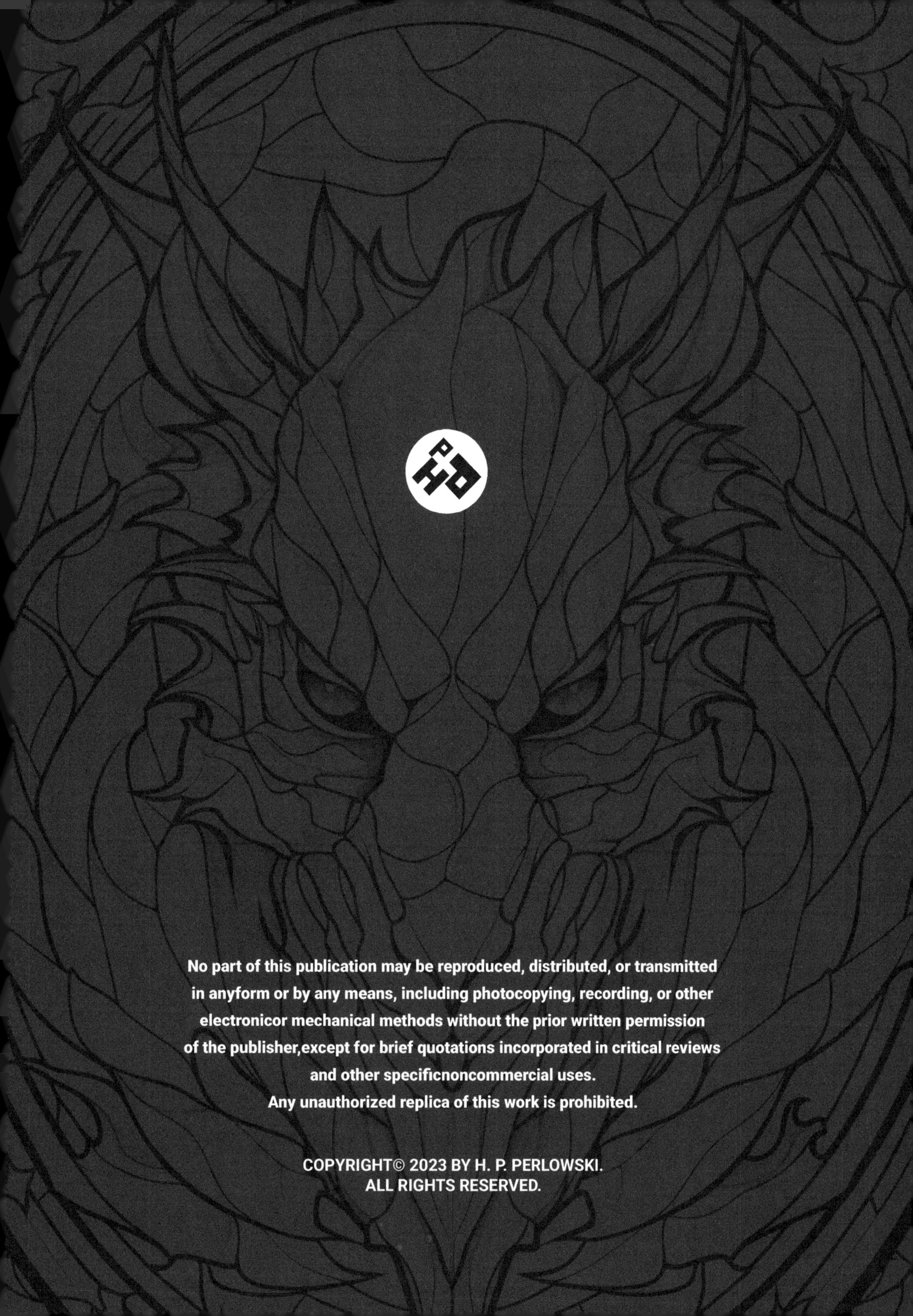

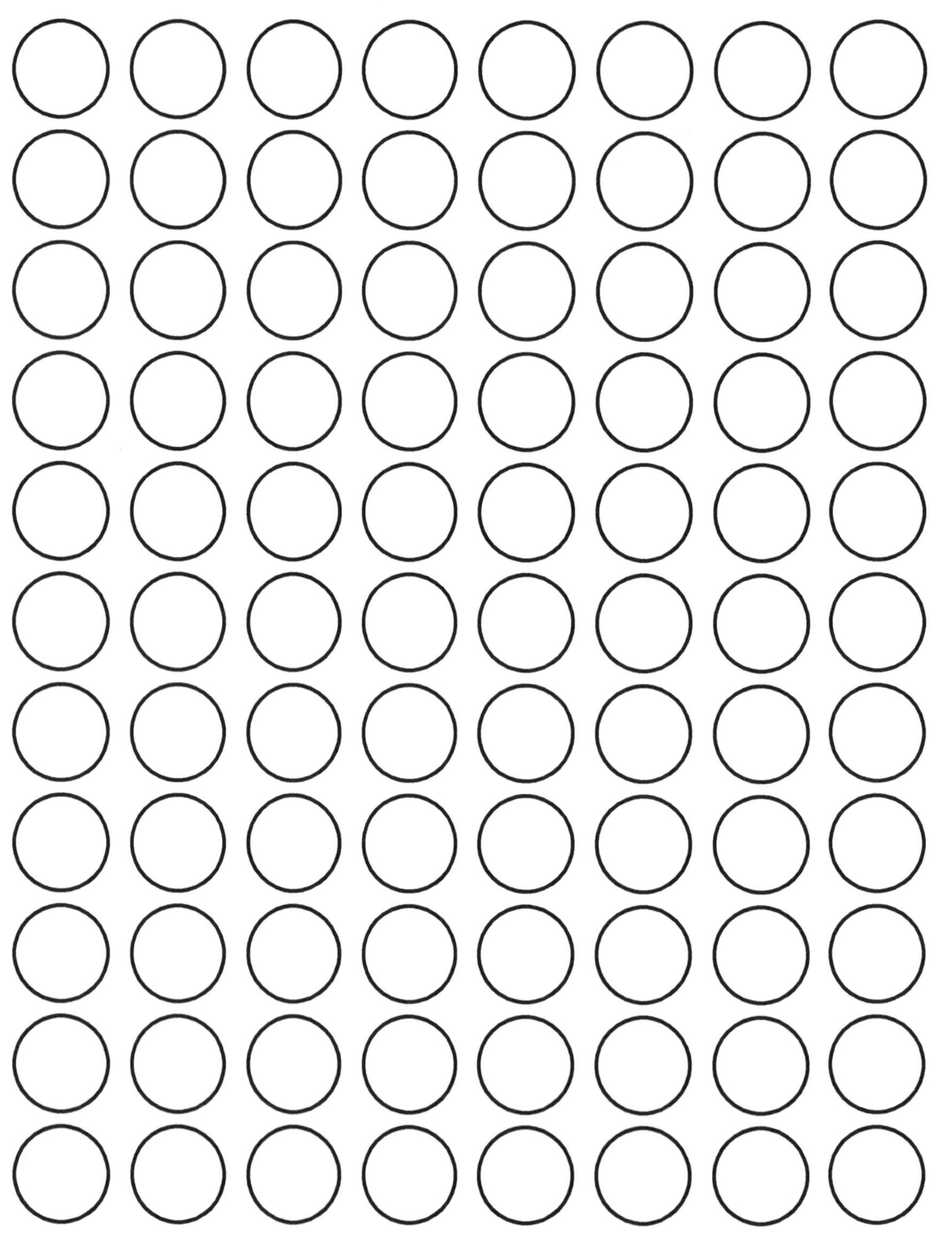

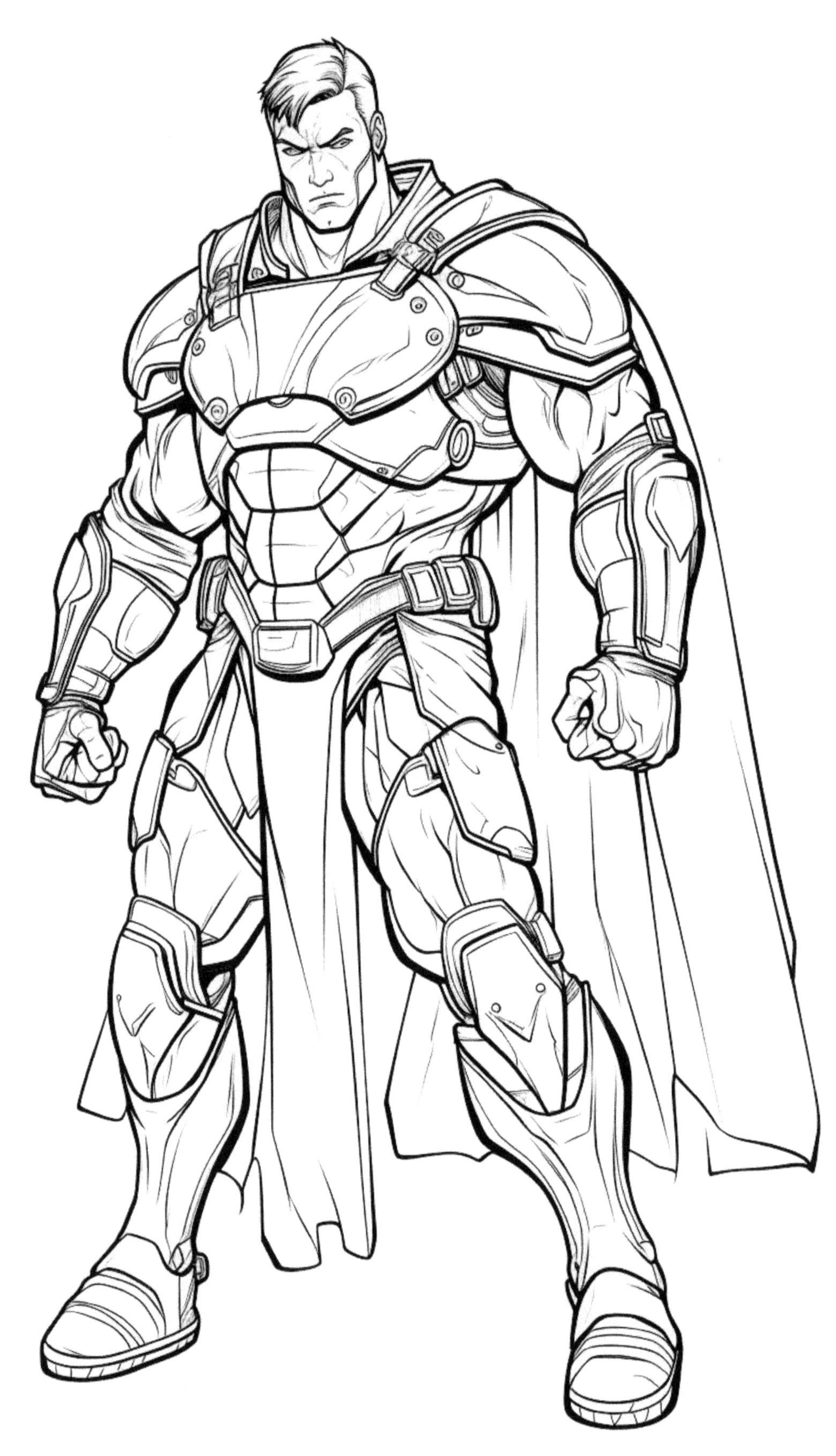

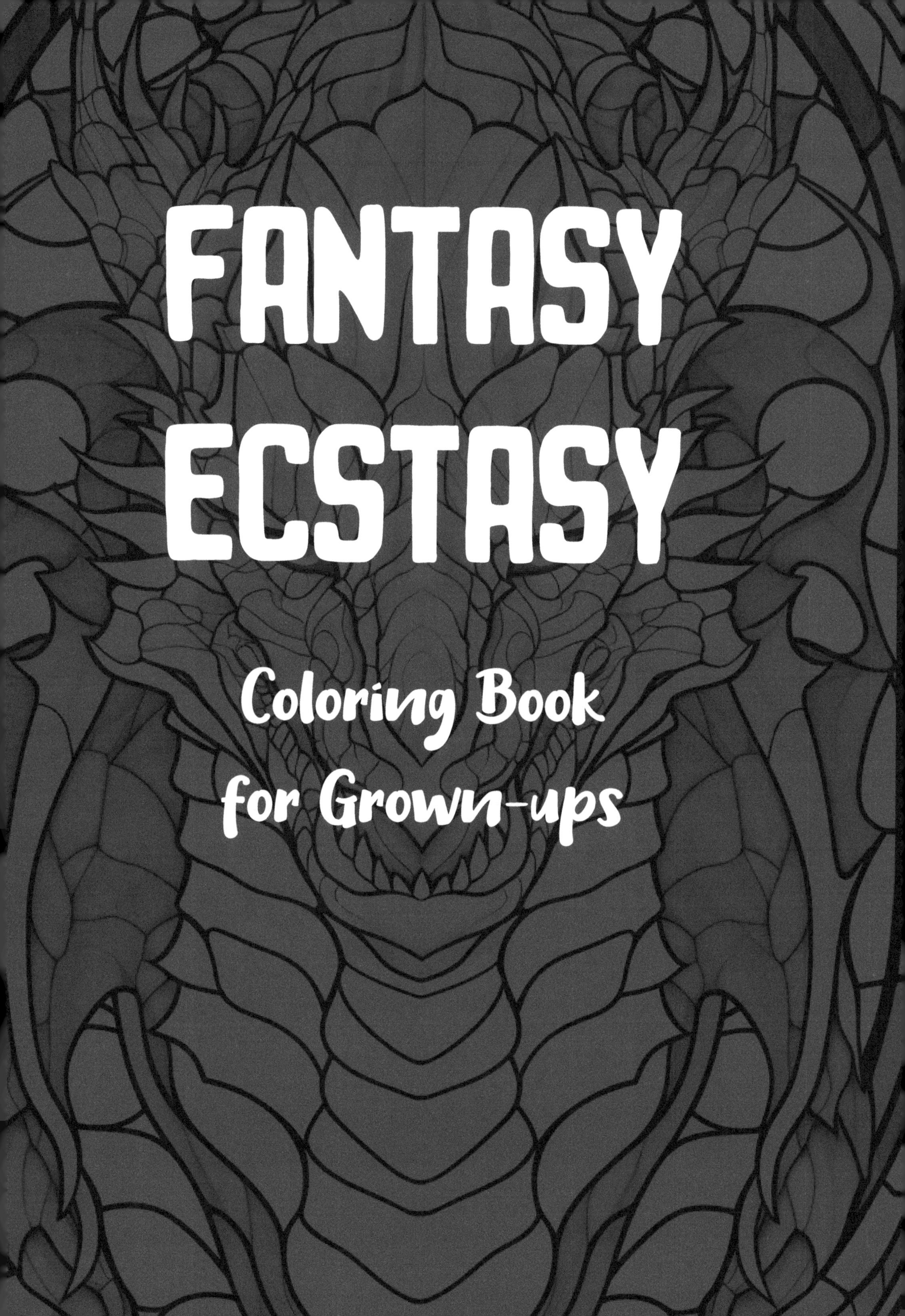

FANTASY
ECSTASY
Coloring Book
for Grown-ups

We hope You enjoy it. Bye.